In my photographs of Big Bend National Park, I have tried to express the harmony and solitude that I feel present in its environs. Although the park is an immense one, there is an intimacy in the small nooks and crannies which pepper the area. These are the secret places that many may pass but few will recognize. My satisfaction stems from the discovery of these "hidden" spots along a trail rather than from following the markers leading to the main attractions. In such a harsh and demanding environment, there are shapes and forms of an exquisite and ephemeral beauty. Light and shadow mold this desert landscape. A shadow can take on a life of its own, like a giant creature floating over the earth. Or a wall of rock can suddenly glow with a soft, shimmering radiance. These secret places emanate a presence, a mood that makes them special.

R.A.H.

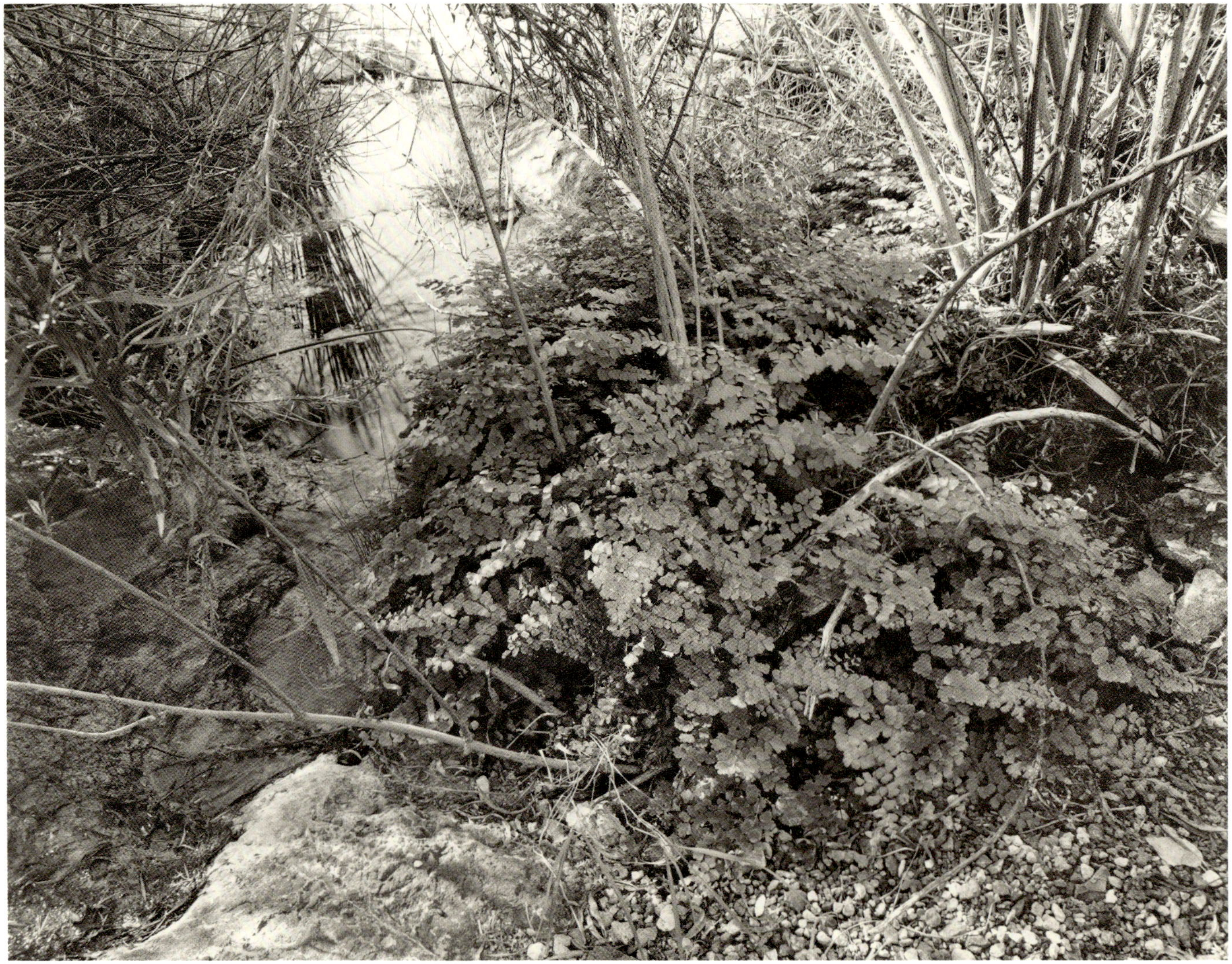

2 | ferns at a desert spring

wilderness waterfall

rocky wash

mesquite shadows

madrone

cottonwood

tuff and magma

river sunset

10 | Basin sunrise

Window pouroff

12 | limestone cliff—
Hot Springs

end of the trail—
Pine Canyon

Mule Ears Spring

wind-blown tamarisk

16 cholla and sotol

sand bar—Rio Grande

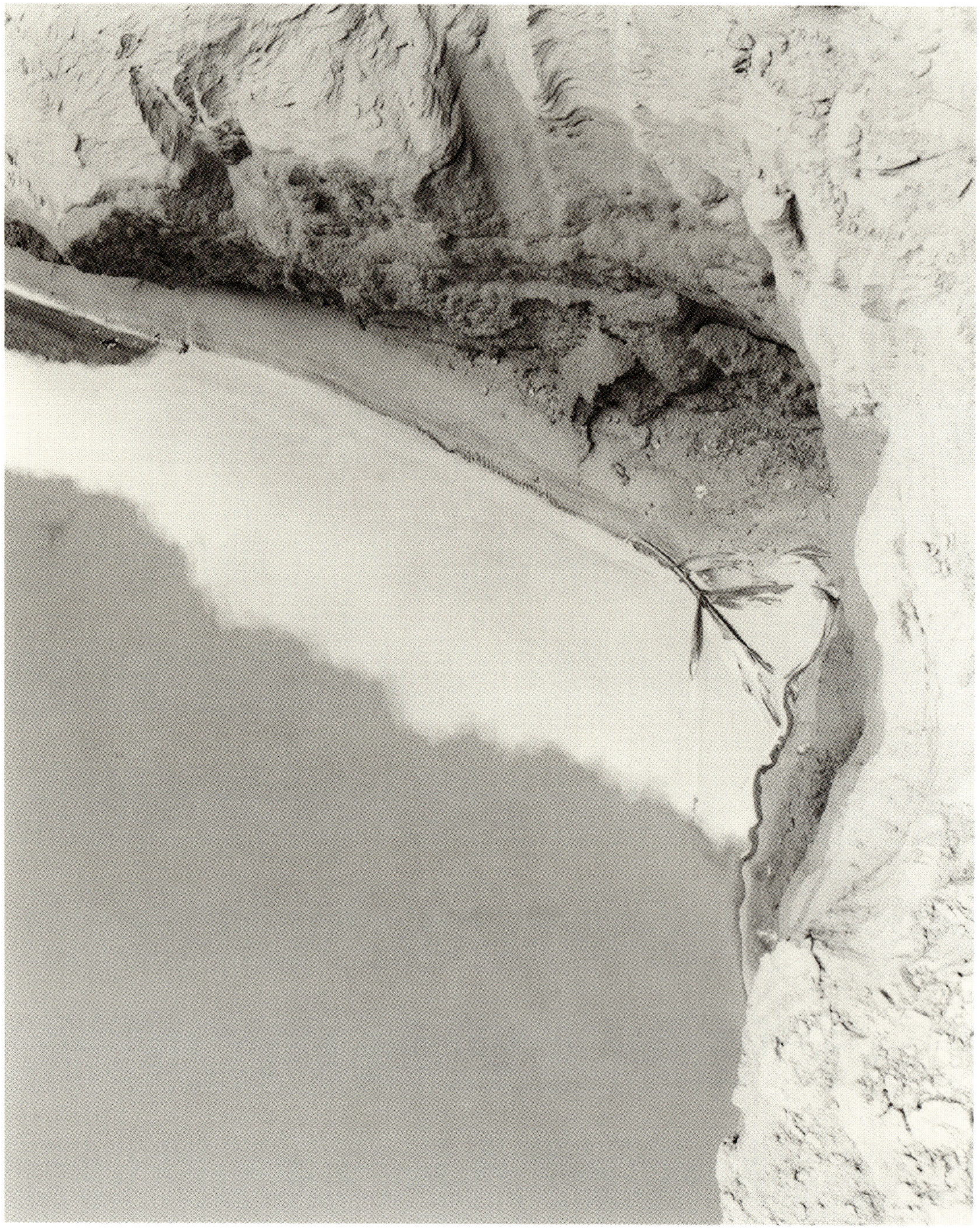

river reflection

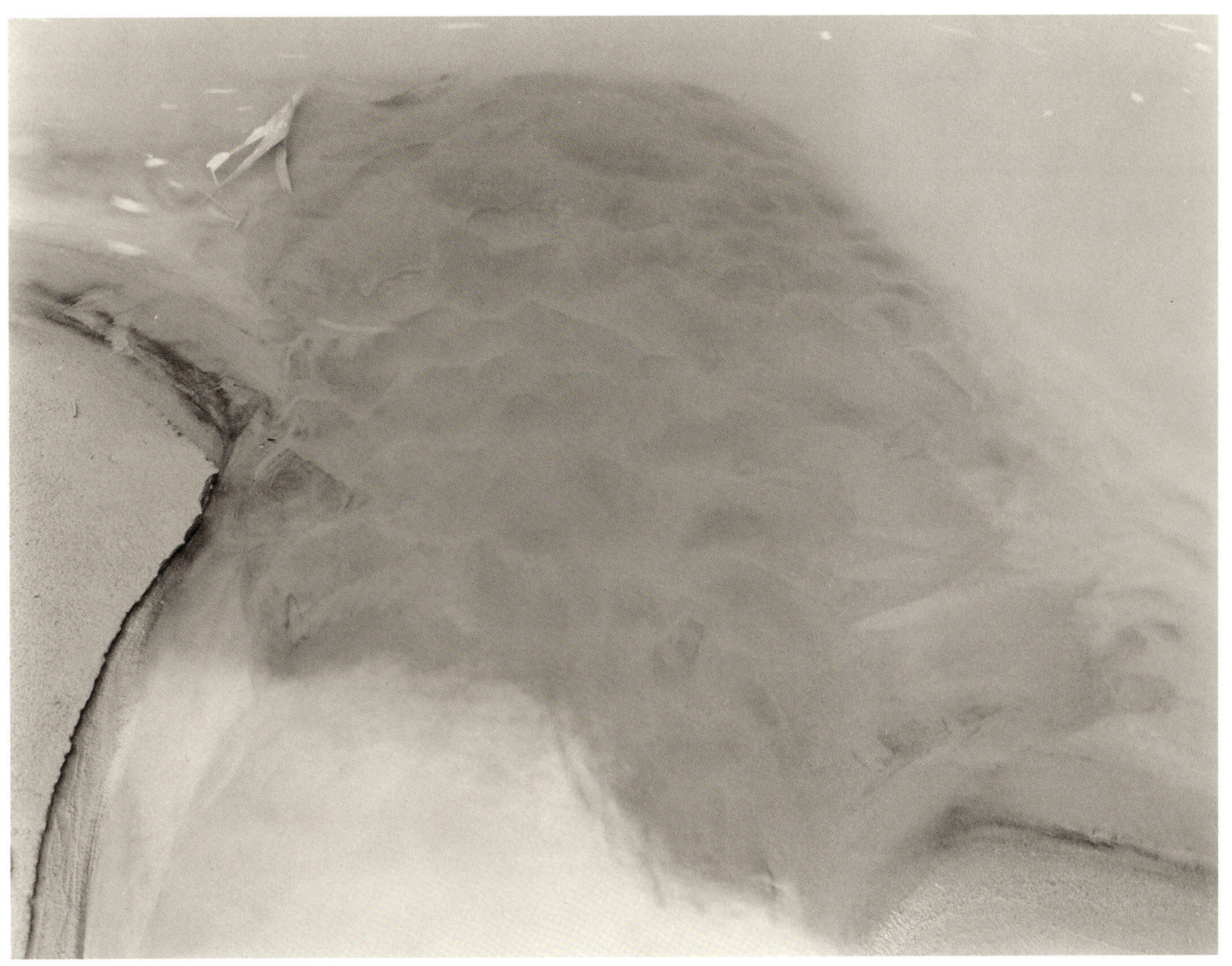

Crown Mountain and
ponderosa pine

end of the trail—
Pine Canyon

22 | mesquite, sand, and stone

Castolon volcanic area

Maria's cross—Castolon

adobe ruin

26 tuff and lava rock—
Castolon volcanic area

boulders and tuff—
Castolon volcanic area | 27

28 Burro Mesa and clouds

misty mountains

30 | Burro Mesa Pouroff

morning shadow—
Dog Canyon

32 | Rio Grande—
Santa Elena Canyon